Manfred Fettinger

A survey of probabilistic algorithms

GRIN - Verlag für akademische Texte

Der GRIN Verlag mit Sitz in München hat sich seit der Gründung im Jahr 1998 auf die Veröffentlichung akademischer Texte spezialisiert.

Die Verlagswebseite www.grin.com ist für Studenten, Hochschullehrer und andere Akademiker die ideale Plattform, ihre Fachtexte, Studienarbeiten, Abschlussarbeiten oder Dissertationen einem breiten Publikum zu präsentieren.

Manfred Fettinger

A survey of probabilistic algorithms

GRIN Verlag

Bibliografische Information der Deutschen Nationalbibliothek: Die Deutsche Bibliothek verzeichnet diese Publikation in der Deutschen Nationalbibliografie; detaillierte bibliografische Daten sind im Internet über http://dnb.d-nb.de/ abrufbar.

1. Auflage 2009
Copyright © 2009 GRIN Verlag
http://www.grin.com/
Druck und Bindung: Books on Demand GmbH, Norderstedt Germany
ISBN 978-3-640-26852-8

FH Technikum Wien

Bachelor Thesis

A survey of prohabilistic algorithms

Written by Manfred Fettinger

Vienna, 14.1.2009

Written at University of Applied Sciences Technikum Vienna
Study Programme BICSS

Kurzfassung

Probabilistische Algorithmen sind in der IT noch nicht weit verbreitet. Oft ist die probabilistische Variante die einzige Möglichkeit überhaupt Probleme zu lösen. Man findet viele wissenschaftliche Arbeiten darüber, jedoch fehlt eine Arbeit die den Einstieg in die Materie erleichtert und mit anschaulichen Beispielen dokumentiert. Diese Arbeit fasst andere Arbeiten auf diesem Gebiet zusammen und vergleicht verschiedene Anwendungen für ähnliche Problemstellungen. Weiters wird ein Überblick über die Funktionsweise von probabilistischen Algorithmen gegeben und drei Anwendungsgebiete vorgestellt. In dieser Arbeit werden probabilistische Datenbanken, Routing und Broadcast beschrieben und verschiedene Varianten verglichen.

Schlagwörter: Probabilistischer Broadcast, Probabilistiches Routing, Probabilistischer Broadcast, Gossiping, Zufall

Abstract

Probabilistic algorithms in IT are not yet wide spread. Often probabilistic variants are the only feasible solution for problems. You can find many papers about them, but there is a lack of a paper which initiates you into this domain and helps to understand it with many demonstrative examples. The contribution of this paper is to summarize information of different papers and compare different applications for same problems. Furthermore to present how and why probabilistic algorithms work. In this paper probabilistic databases, routing and broadcasting are described and different variants compared.

Keywords: probabilistic broadcast, probabilistic routing, probabilistic databases, gossiping, randomization

Acknowledgements

Thanks to Kenneth P. Birman from the Cornell University in Ithaca for giving the permission to use figures from his paper [1] as well as Avri Doria from the Electronics and Telecommunications Research Institute of Korea to use figures out of [7].

Table of Contents

1 Introduction

We all learn about computers that there are only two states 0 and 1. If we start a program to compute anything we expect an exact result. And now there should be applications which use probability to calculate results? How should this work?

First of all we distinguish a deterministic from a probabilistic algorithm. Deterministic means that the result of an operation is predictable. As an example we imagine two machines. The first machine in figure 1a is a deterministic machine which will always produce sin(x) as output for a given input x. At figure 1b we see a probabilistic machine which will calculate sin(x) with a probability P=0,8 and cos(x) with a probability P=0,2. Therefore a user can go for sure when using a deterministic machine and x=90 he will always get 1 as output. When using the probabilistic machine, with a probability of 80% he will get 1 and with a probability of 20% he will get 0 as output.

Fig. 1: A deterministic a) and a probabilistic machine b)

It cannot be said that one of them is better than the other, each approach has its areas where it performs best. The overall difference of them is if you need an algorithm that executes a task with a very high reliability then we are talking about the deterministic variant. Is the target something else then the probabilistic approach may performs better. Of course there are many tasks where you would need a high reliable solution but it is not possible to use a deterministic variant e.g. through lack of needed infrastructure. But this does not mean that probabilistic variants are unreliable and deterministic variants are reliable. A deterministic algorithm depends also on probabilities but they have not so much impact as they have at probabilistic algorithms. If we imagine a calculator and we want to calculate sin(90) there is also a possibility that the calculator runs out of battery or an error occurs on the printing board due to a bad soldering and therefore we do not get the result we are expecting.

As [9] points out, using randomization in design and analysis of algorithms has several advantages. These algorithms are often simpler and more efficient in terms of time, space and communication complexity, than deterministic variants. Also for some problems, mainly in the field of distributed computing and multi-processing, there exist no deterministic one.

But this gain in simplicity, efficiency and solvability has its price. Normally when designing an algorithm an integral part of this is, to assure the correctness. At probabilistic algorithms the sacrifice is to lose the traditional notion of correctness for a quantitative notation – correctness with a probability between 0 and 1 [9].

Probabilistic algorithms often work with a lot of parameters. With them it is possible to control the behaviour of those algorithms. Depending on if performance or reliability is more important these parameters must be suitably set. It is a hard task to find the right settings for your application area, therefore lot of experience and simulation work is necessary. For example let's have a look on such a probabilistic equation like it is used for probabilistic routing in the PRoPHET algorithm described in chapter 3.3.

$$P_{(a,b)} = P_{(a,b)old} + \left(1 - P_{(a,b)old}\right) \times P_{init}$$

The detailed description of this formula is shown later, for explanation reasons we note that $P_{(a,b)}$ describes the probability that node A is able to contact node B. There is also a variable P_{init} which is here the mentioned parameter which has to be set suitably for needed reasons.

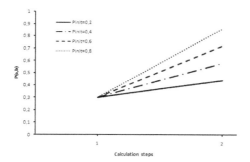

Fig. 2: Comparison of results with different parameter P_{init}

Figure 2 shows the behaviour of the result when P_{init} changes. In this example $P_{(a,b)}$ was initially set to 0,3 and for P_{init} four different values were used. As it can be seen, the result can differ up to 50%. Therefore the same probabilistic algorithm can produce a completely different result when parameters are selected differently.

This paper gives an overview of three different applications where such probabilistic algorithms are used. It will be also shown that in some cases the probabilistic approach is the only feasible solution. The contribution of this paper is to summarize information of different papers and compare different applications for same problems. Furthermore to present how and why probabilistic algorithms work.

The first probabilistic application this paper presents is about probabilistic broadcast protocols. Broadcasting is used whenever information has to spread over a whole network. Deterministic variants like flooding are often not suitable because of performance reasons. Primarily in large area networks or ad-hoc networks this problem often occurs.

Probabilistic routing builds the second part in this paper. Routing is used to find the best way between two nodes in a network. Like in broadcasting there are different approaches whereas probabilistic approaches are often the only feasible because of the same reasons. Also

2

deterministic variants need a fully connected path between communication endpoints but there are scenarios where this is not possible and here probabilistic routing can help.

Last this paper gives you an introduction in probabilistic databases. Normally you can query a database and will get one answer. Probabilistic databases support different possible information for an entity therefore a query will result in different answers with different probabilities. This is suitable for data inputs which are maybe old, false or for integration of data from different sources.

2 Probabilistic broadcast

This chapter describes the probabilistic broadcast/multicast with usage of two different implementations: Lightweight Probabilistic Broadcast and Anonymous Gossiping. For the Lightweight Probabilistic Broadcast most information is taken from [3], for Anonymous Gossiping [1] was used as main source. Information about gossiping was mainly taken from [8].

2.1 Broadcasting

A network consists of a number of nodes which can contact other nodes of the network. Broadcasting is now a task which is used to spread information over the whole network, figure 3 shows this problem where a node with information is colored red. Maybe a node creates a message and wants to spread this message to all other nodes. Therefore there are different approaches available. Flooding [8], Broadcast Tree [8] and Gossiping are algorithms for this task. In this paper we speak about broad- or multicasting where multicasting means that the information is not spread over the whole network but only to a group of nodes in the network which belong together.

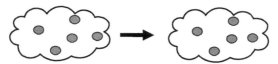

Fig. 3: Broadcasting adapted from [8]

Important parameters for broadcasting an information [8] are reliability (the information should be send to all nodes), speed (the faster the information is spread the better it is), network traffic (less network traffic would reduce consumption of resources), robustness (if a node crashes broadcasting should not be stopped, new nodes should also get the information) and scalability (costs for spreading messages in a growing network should ideally increase linearly).

Two important questions in broadcasting are how the membership management and the message buffering are done [3]. For membership management there are mainly two concepts, the *centralized* where a server maintains all members and the *decentralized* where every node knows about the other members. Unlike the decentralized, the centralized solution leads to problems with limited resources and scales very badly. [3] points out that a decentralized solution with a partial view of the system would be the best choice.

Messages are buffered temporarily at each node until the buffer is full. There are several possibilities to delete messages, [3] mentions a random deletion of messages or a deletion after n rounds.

2.2 Gossiping

Gossiping is a technique which has its history in human behaviour and dissemination of diseases. It uses the idea of epidemic behaviour which describes the propagation of diseases in nature where in short time many of individuals become infected. In the epidemic behaviour there are three states shown in figure 4. Nodes with the state susceptible are nodes which don't have the information. Nodes get infected when they get the message or information. After a concrete condition (times of infections, if contacted node has already the information) the node stops message dissemination and gets into the state removed. This fact is like it is in real diseases. There an individual is infected with a virus, then it infects other individuals until it gets healed and is immune against this virus or dies due to the consequences of the virus.

Susceptible   Infected   Removed

Fig. 4: SIR Model adapted from [8]

The same behaviour can also be seen at humans when the spread rumors. [12] tells as example that somebody has information and wants to tell this to his friends. Therefore he calls Tony to tell him the news. Tony then calls Lisa and so on. Now when Tony calls Tom and Tom tells him that he already heard the news, Tony will stop spreading this information. And this is the way gossiping works.

Gossiping can be done in different variations [8] generally we differentiate between "infect forever" where a node spreads the information forever and "infect and die" where the information is disseminated until a condition is reached. To implement a gossiping algorithm there are different questions [8]:

Does the sender node get feedback from the receiver node?

- Blind
  Sending node gets no feedback from receiver node
- Feedback
  Sending node gets feedback from receiver

At the blind-concept therefore it is not possible for the sender node to decide to stop dissemination if the receiver node was already informed. Unlike the blind-concept at the feedback-concept the sender gets informed about the receiver's state. Thus it is possible at the feedback approach to let nodes stop dissemination if the receiver node was already informed.

When does the infected node stop dissemination?

- Coin
  Dissemination is stopped with a probability of $\frac{1}{k}$
- Counter
  Dissemination is stopped after k steps

In this concept an internal parameter k is used as criteria when message spreading is stopped. At the coin-concept the parameter is used for a probabilistic, at the counter-concept it is used for a deterministic criteria.

Which node does inform?

When a node randomly selects another, there are different possibilities for exchanging messages.

- Push
  Sender node pushes information to receiver
- Pull
  Sender pulls information from receiver
- Push/Pull
  Sender and receiver exchange messages

2.3 Lightweight Probabilistic Broadcast

The fist application which is presented is the Lightweight Probabilistic Broadcast (LPBCAST). This chapter explains how it works and where the probabilistic behaviour is located. Later LPBCAST is compared to a different algorithm for probabilistic broadcasting – anonymous gossiping.

2.3.1 Overview

LPBCAST as described in [3] is a probabilistic broadcast algorithm which relies on following facts:

- Partial views
- Periodic gossip messages
- No need of an underlying protocol
- Every node has a view size l and sends gossip messages to F nodes

Figure 5 shows the overall view of a multicast group. In this group the red colored node has information it wants to disseminate. This node has only a partial view of the whole group (blue rectangle), the size l of this view is 4. The node does not know the other nodes of the group.

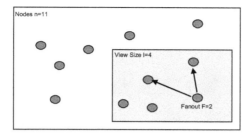

Fig. 5: A multicast group showing a node with information (red)

Furthermore this node randomly selects two nodes of its partial view for message dissemination. The Fanout F indicates the number of nodes to which the information is spread inside the view. It is clear that $F <= l <= n$ where n indicates the number of all nodes of the multicast group.

2.3.2 The gossip message

The gossip message contains information shown in figure 6.

Fig. 6: Gossip message in LPBCAST

The message contains [3] all *event notifications* the node received, since the last outgoing gossip message was sent. Also it contains *event notification ids* of all events the node has ever received. To update the view of every node the message also carries a set of *subscriptions* and *unsubscriptions* from its individual view so that every receiving node can update its own view.

2.3.3 Procedures

Overall the LPBCAST algorithm consists of two main procedures [3]. One starts periodically to send gossip messages, the other starts whenever a gossip message is received.

Reception of a gossip message [3]

When a gossip message is received by a node first of all it updates its own view by handling all unsubscriptions and subscriptions the message contains. Then it delivers all event notifications to the application if they are new to the node.

Gossiping (periodically) [3]

Every node generates periodically a gossip message shown in figure 6 and sends it to F other nodes of its partial view. If there are no new event notifications to disseminate, it even sends a

gossip message to exchange digests and keep the view updated. This fact also results in an overall network load and avoids fluctuations of network traffic.

Retrieving event notification ids through gossip [3]

When the receiver node gets the information through the event notification ids of the gossip message that there exists an event notification it has not received yet, it stores the id of the event notification, the current round number[1] and the process ID of the source into a buffer. Then the node waits a given number of rounds before it starts fetching the event notification from another node. Also another test is done to check if the event was received during waiting from another gossip message. If the event was not received yet, the node asks the node from which it received the event notification id. If the event notification cannot be received from this node, a random node from its view is asked for it. If that also fails then the original sender of the event notification is asked.

Subscription and unsubscription of processes [3]

If a node N1 wants to join the system it has to know another node N2 which is already member of the group. N1 sends then a subscription to N2 and due to dissemination of gossip messages, the subscription will gradually be added to the system. If the subscription was correct, N1 will notice this by receiving more and more gossip messages. Otherwise a timeout triggers the re-emission of the subscription.

When a node wants to leave, it will be gradually removed from the individual views of the nodes of the system. To avoid that unsubscriptions remain forever in the system a timestamp is used.

2.3.4 Analytical evaluation

In this section it is shown how the probability is calculated and how different parameters effect the dissemination. First the probability that a given node N2 belongs to the individual view of a node N1 is [3]:

$$P = \frac{l}{(n-1)}$$

Where l indicates the view size and n the total number of nodes in the system. Now it is interesting what is the lower bound on the probability that a given node is infected (gets the information) by a gossip message [3]. Therefore we need two more predefined constants which are the probability for a message loss ε and the probability that a node crashes during a run τ.

$$P = \left(\frac{l}{(n-1)}\right)\left(\frac{F}{l}\right)(1-\varepsilon)(1-\tau)$$
$$\quad (1) \qquad (2) \quad (3) \quad (4)$$

---

[1] round number means the current round in event dissemination

This formula indicates the probability that

1. Node is known by the sender
2. Node is chosen as target
3. Message is not lost
4. Target node does not crash

By considering that both parameters ε and τ are beyond the limits of our influence, the only deterministic factors to analyze are the fanout F and the system size n [3]. The view size l has no impact to the performance due to the fact it can be cut from above equation. Figure 7 shows the relation between the number of rounds needed to broadcast a message to a system of 125 nodes.

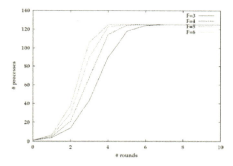

Fig. 7: Expected number of infected processes with different fanout values copied from [3]

This figure shows that with increasing fanout the number of rounds decreases. The hard task is to find a good value for fanout because if a fanout is chosen too high it results in redundant messages and overloads the network [3].

In figure 8 the impact of the system size n is shown in relation to the number of rounds needed to infect 99% of a system. The figure points out that the number of rounds increases logarithmically with an increasing system size [3].

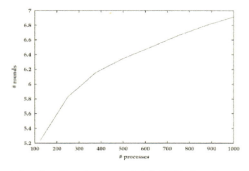

Fig. 8: Expected number of rounds necessary to infect 99% of a system copied from [3]

2.4 Anonymous gossiping

Anonymous gossiping (AG) is the second algorithm presented for probabilistic broadcasting. It will now be explained as LBPCAST before and compared against it. Afterwards most important differences between them are pointed out.

2.4.1 Overview

AG was mainly invented for the use in mobile ad-hoc networks where no fixed infrastructure is available [1]. In comparison to LPBCAST it has the following attributes

- No periodical messages are needed to update a view
- Nodes exchange information outside the normal message delivery phase
- No member needs to know other members of the group
- An underlying multicast protocol is required (e.g. MAODV[2])
- Membership management is done by the underlying protocol

Due to the fact that AG uses an underlying protocol it is necessary to explain how a protocol as MAODV [11] works. Each node maintains two routing tables called the Route Table (RT) which records the next hop for routes to other nodes. It consists of following fields: destination ip, destination sequence number, hop count to destination, ip of next hop and a TTL[3]-Field. The second table is called Multicast Route Table (MRT) and contains entries for multicast groups: Multicast group ip, group leader ip, group sequence number, hop count to group leader, next hops containing the nodes in the tree to which actual node is connected and also a TTL-Field. Furthermore MAODV maintains a multicast tree for each group, a leaf node member can leave the group without any restrictions but if a non leaf node wants to leave the group it must continue to function as a router in the tree [11].

2.4.2 The gossip message

The gossip message [1] differs from the one which is used in LPBCAST, also due to the fact an underlying protocol is needed. Figure 9 shows the message in detail.

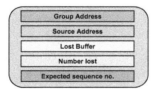

Fig. 9: Gossip message in anonymous gossiping

The *group address* contains the address of the multicast group, the *source address* holds the address of the sender node, the *lost buffer* (an array) contains sequence numbers of messages the node has not got, the field *number lost* contains the number of missing messages (number

---

[2] Multicast Ad-hoc On-demand Distance Vector Routing [11]

[3] Time To Life

of entries in the lost buffer) and the *expected sequence number* holds the next message that the node expects.

2.4.3 Procedures

A node randomly selects one of its neighbours (it knows them from the above mentioned routing tables of MAODV) and sends a gossip message to it. If a node receives a gossip message it depends whether or not it is a member of the group or acts only as a router. Group members randomly decide to accept the message or propagate it to another node (excluding the sender). If the receiver is a router-node it only propagates it to a neighbour of it. When a node accepts the gossip message it replies to the sender and starts gossiping with it. Figure 10 shows this behaviour.

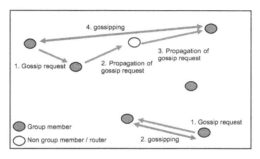

Fig. 10: The procedure of gossiping in anonymous gossiping

The locality of gossiping is also very important because a gossip with a nearer member will reduce network traffic but also gossiping with distant nodes is very important because in the case of a crash a whole locality could be affected and the message would be forever lost. Therefore [1] suggest a scheme where gossiping with locally nodes occurs with high probability and with distant nodes only occasionally. This scheme will hold the network traffic acceptable and avoid message loss. That this is possible each node maintains an additional field called *nearest_member* which is associated with a nexthop [1]. In MAODV the MRT is extended with this field. It contains the distance to the nearest group member from the actual node through this nexthop. Now a nexthop with a smaller *nearest_member* value is chosen with higher probability than one with a larger value. For better understanding figure 11 shows an example.

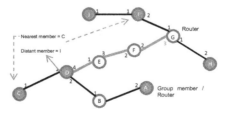

Fig. 11: Network showing the usage of the nearest_member value adapted from [1]

The number next to the edge of a node contains the number of hops to the nearest member through this edge. For example node G needs 3 hops over the redlined edge to the nearest member of the group. If a node wants to leave or join the group the nearest neighbour will realize this event and adjust its MRT.

Anonymous gossiping also uses a cache to improve performance [1]. As you can see in figure 10 gossiping is done by unicast if a node accepts the gossip message. This information is then stored in the member_cache. The member cache contains 3-tuples (*node_addr, numhops, last_gossip*). The field *node_addr* contains the address of a group member, *numhops* is the shortest distance between the nodes and *last_gossip* contains the time when the last gossip with this node was done. But the *member_cache* is not always used, the following algorithm decides whether the cache is used or not. At each round a node chooses to do anonymous gossiping with probability *p*. If AG is chosen, then gossiping is done without using the cache. Otherwise cached gossiping is chosen, then a member is selected randomly from the *member_cache* and the message is unicast to it.

2.4.4 Analytical evaluation

For a performance analysis figure 12 was taken from [1] to see how AG performs against normal usage of MAODV. It shows that anonymous gossiping performs better than MAODV when keeping the average number of neighbours approximately constant. Also it's easy to see that with increasing number of nodes in the network the number of delivered packets decreases. This is because with increasing nodes the routing distance between the nodes goes up and therefore the number of link failures also increases [1].

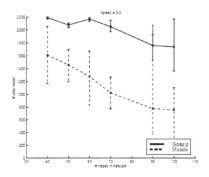

Fig. 12: Packet delivery vs. number of nodes copied from [1]

2.5 Comparison

As described before there are several differences between LPBCAST and AG. Table 1 lists the differences which are most important.

	LPBCAST	AG
Need of underlying protocol	No	Yes
Nodes member information	Partial view	Neighbours
Gossip receiver	Random – of partial view	With high probability near group member with low probability distant group member
Number of receivers per round	As defined in fanout	1
Recognition of locality	No	Yes
Caching used	No	Yes
Age-based message purging	Yes	No

Table 1: Comparison of LPBCAST and AG

2.6 Practical scenarios

Mentioned algorithms are designed for use in large scaling and ad-hoc networks where the infrastructure and topology can change. [3] mentions that probabilistic broadcasting algorithms are ideal candidates to support peer-to-peer applications. There are also papers [5] about gossiping in peer-to-peer systems. Therefore it can be assumed that such algorithms are used in such systems.

3 Probabilistic routing

After probabilistic broadcasting, this chapter is about probabilistic and epidemic routing used in intermittently connected networks where a connected path between source and destination node is not always given. Probabilistic broadcasting and routing have similar characteristics due to the fact that both are used for information dissemination. Main source for probabilistic routing was [7], for epidemic routing [13] was used.

3.1 Routing

Routing is used in networks if the transmission is connection oriented and a node wants to send a message to another one in the network. Therefore a path must be found to the destination node. This should be done in a fast way without using too many hops.

3.2 Epidemic routing

Epidemic routing is not a real probabilistic routing protocol because it does not calculate any probabilities for its decision for selecting nodes. A distinction to deterministic variants is only given by the fact that a node receives a message only probably. But it is mentioned here to point out the differences to a real probabilistic approach (chapter 3.3).

Epidemic routing relies on the epidemic behaviour as described in chapter 2. It also relies upon transitive distribution of messages. Epidemic routing should deliver a message with high probability to a particular host. The goals of epidemic routing [13] are to maximize the message delivery rate and minimize the delivery latency and the needed resources which are consumed in message delivery. This is reached by upper bounds on the message hop count which means that the used nodes between source and destination are limited. Moreover the node buffer space is bounded so that a node can only hold a limited number of messages. This leads to the fact that increasing of bounds results in increasing the probability of successful delivery in exchange for higher resource consumption [13].

3.2.1 Procedures

Whenever two nodes get into communication range a node is contacting the other. This could be e.g. by comparing the IDs [13] and the node with the smaller ID starts an anti-entropy-session. Such anti-entropy-session is shown in figure 13. Each node maintains a *summary_vector* which contains the keys of the messages a node stores.

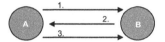

Fig. 13: Anti-entropy-session adapted from [13]

First node A contacts node B and sends it *summary_vector* to node B (1). Node B then creates a new vector holding the messages it needs from node's A *summary_vector* and send this vector back to A (2). Last node A transmits the requested messages to B (3). If node B later gets in contact with another node this anti-entropy session is repeated transitively [13].

Important to know is that epidemic routing exchanges messages with every node in its communication range. For a better understanding of the transitive behaviour figure 14 shows an example where a source node S want to send a message to the destination node D. All other nodes in the network act then as carrier-nodes C. The dotted circles mark the communication range.

Fig. 14: Transitive behaviour in epidemic routing adapted from [13]

First two nodes are in communication range of S, therefore S transmits the message to both nodes. Later node C_2 came into the range of C_3 and transmits also the message to it. C_3 is still in range of D and delivers the message to the destination node D.

3.3 Probabilistic routing using PRoPHET[4]

This implementation uses the fact that nodes do not move around randomly, instead the movement is predictable through behavioural patterns [7]. Therefore it is possible to set probabilities for movements. If you imagine animals in the wilderness there is maybe a cave where they have their home, also they are often in an area where they are hunting and there is a place on the near river where they drink. Thus it is understandable that the probability that such animal moves between this areas is very high. On the other hand you must be lucky to see this animal elsewhere.

PRoPHET, other than epidemic routing, gossips messages only to suitable nodes. These are nodes where the probability is high, when using it for routing, the message will arrive at the destination node. PRoPHET uses historical information of encounters and transitivity of nodes to calculate probabilities of suitable nodes [7]. The goal of PRoPHET is to minimize messages and therefore reduce the consumption of resources [7]. This is reached by sending the messages only to suitable nodes.

To accomplish this [7] creates a probabilistic metric called delivery predictability $P_{(a,b)} \in [0,1]$, which indicates the probability that node A is able to deliver a message to node B. Moreover every node holds two vectors. The *delivery predictability vector* holds the delivery predictability information, the *summary vector* contains an index of all stored messages [7].

3.3.1 Procedures

When two nodes get into communication range they exchange their both vectors and update their own predictability vector with the information from the other nodes predictability vector. The message is then only sent to the other node if the delivery predictability for the destination node is higher than the own entry. The node which transmits the message to the other node keeps the message as long there is enough buffer space available. If the buffer is full when a new message is received, a message is deleted from buffer according to the queue management system [7].

3.3.2 Calculating the delivery predictability

In the following, it is described how PRoPHET calculates its probabilities. First whenever a node is encountered the probability of delivery ability to this node is increasing [7]. This is done by following formula:

$$P_{(a,b)} = P_{(a,b)old} + \left(1 - P_{(a,b)old}\right) \times P_{init}$$

In this formula P_{init} describes an initialization constant. [7] used 0,75 for it. Figure 15 visualizes the change of the probabilities when two nodes meet.

---

[4] Probabilistic Routing Protocol using History of Encounters and Transitivity

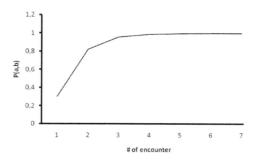

Fig. 15: Probability increasing when nodes encounter

In this example P_{init} was set to 0,75. Also it was assumed that node A has an initial delivery predictability to B of 30%. It figures out that the probability increases rapidly whenever two nodes encounter. After the first contact the figures change only slightly.

The second calculation is to decrease the probability of less encountered nodes. Also it must be ensured that the delivery predictability of a node A to node B that have not encountered node B in a predefined time must decrease [7]. That means the delivery predictability must age. Following formula decreases the probability:

$$P_{(a,b)} = P_{(a,b)old} \times \gamma^k$$

Where k describes the time units elapsed since the last time of aging and $\gamma \in [0,1]$ stands for an aging constant. Figure 16 emphasizes the results of this equation where the initial value of $P_{(a,b)}$ was set to 0,99.

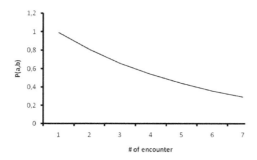

Fig. 16: Probability decreasing at aging

In the aging calculation γ=0,98 (as mentioned in [7]) and k=10. It can be seen that at aging the decrease of probability values is slower than they increase when nodes meet.

Last the transitive property must also be considered [7]. The transitive property means if node A often encounters B and B often encounters C, then node B is a good carrier for messages from A to C or backwards. Following equation ensures that this property is considered:

$$P_{(a,c)} = P_{(a,c)old} + (1 - P_{(a,c)old}) \times P_{(a,b)} \times P_{(b,c)} \times \beta$$

In this equation $\beta \in [0,1]$ is a scaling constant which controls the impact of transitivity. Also here figure 17 shows how figures are changing:

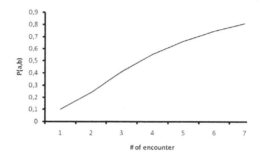

Fig. 17: Probability increasing at transitive property

This example shows that the probability is constantly increasing. Here for $P_{(a,b)}$ an initial delivery predictability of 70%, for $P_{(a,c)}$ of 10% and for $P_{(b,c)}$ of 90% was assumed. The value of β was set to 0,25. Furthermore it is assumed that at every round nodes A-B and B-C meet and increases their predictability vector. It points out that the transitivity like aging increases widely linear.

3.3.3 Simulation

For a better understanding figure 18 shows a simulation of the transitive behaviour of PRoPHET. Also the delivery predictability vector is shown in every subfigure.

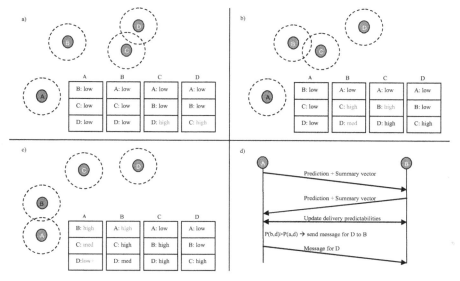

Fig. 18: Transitive behaviour with delivery predictabilities adapted from [7]

In figure 18a) you can see that A holds a message which it wants to transmit to node D. Also C and D are in communication range, therefore the probability that C meets D and backwards increases. In 18b) B and C meet, they increase their probability furthermore B uses the transitive property and sets the probability for D to medium. The same happens in 18c) where A notices that B has a higher probability to send a message to D and so it decides to transmit the message to B. This can be seen in figure 18d).

3.4 Comparison

The fundamental difference between epidemic routing and PRoPHET is the fact that PRoPHET sends messages only to suitable nodes where epidemic routing transmits the messages to every node it encounters. In my opinion epidemic routing is not a fully probabilistic algorithm because there is no probability used in routing. The only distinction to a deterministic approach is the fact, that a node receives a message only probably. Parameters to handle this are as mentioned the buffer size and the hop count. On the other hand PRoPHET is fully probabilistic, it calculates probabilities for every node it encounters and due to the transitive behaviour it also can calculate probabilities for nodes it has never meet.

3.4.1 Experimental results

[7] presents results of simulations made in two scenarios regarding the epidemic routing vs. PRoPHET. First a community scenario where an area is divided into 11 communities and a gathering place. In every community there is a fixed communication node, also in the gathering place. The other is the random scenario where 50 nodes placed randomly over the area and they move according to the random waypoint mobility model [4]. There were made

simulations with different queue size against received messages, delay and number of forwarded messages.

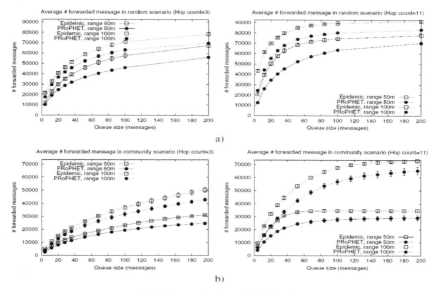

Fig. 19: Communication overhead. a) random
b) community scenario copied from [7]

Only one result is shown in this paper, all others can be found at [7] as well the exact description of the simulation. Due to the fact that the most important difference between both protocols are the number of forwarded messages figure 19 was taken from [7]. It can be easily seen that PRoPHET sends fewer messages than epidemic routing this is no wonder due to PRoPHET sends messages only to suitable nodes whereas epidemic routing does this whenever a node is encountered.

3.5 Practical scenarios

Mentioned probabilistic algorithms for intermittently connected networks are used in regions where no infrastructure is always available. Some examples [7] are:

Project "ZebraNet"

A project where movement of the wildlife in a part in Africa is studied. Therefore zebras were equipped with tracking collars.

Weather monitoring in national parks

In some parks weather monitoring boards were installed which display the weather from another part of the park. For this reason hikers were equipped with small network devices. Due to their mobility through the park the information can be spread above the entire park.

Regions without network infrastructure

The saami population of Sweden had no infrastructure available in their summer camps. Nevertheless they need connection to the internet. For that reason snowmobiles and all terrain vehicles were attached with mobile relays.

Also the DakNet project connected villages in India and Cambodia through relays on buses and motorcycles.

4 Probabilistic databases

Chapters 2 and 3 were about probabilistic broadcasting and routing. These applications are very similar. To give an example of a completely different application for the usage of probability in IT, this chapter describes how probability can be used in databases. Information was mainly taken from [2], [6] and [14].

4.1 Overview

The world consists of many uncertainties but most databases reflect only one true world. If we query a database we get only one or more exact answers. A query like "SELECT * FROM students WHERE personID = 4711" will result in an answer like shown in table 2.

ID	Name	Birth date	City
4711	Manfred	04.10.1975	Vienna

Table 2: Example for a query-result on a deterministic database

But often there are scenarios where we are not sure which information is correct or with which probability it is correct. As example we can imagine data integration from two different sources to a single database where some tuples have the same key but different attribute values. Or as mentioned in [10] to use probabilistic databases for RFID[5] data management. Furthermore it is possible that there is old data in a database stored and not corrected, instead a new tuple was created.

4.2 Possible worlds

In relational databases normally the model of only one world is stored. Probabilistic databases, other than deterministic databases, store more different worlds [2], [14]. Table 3 shows how different worlds are stored in relational databases.

---

[5] Radio Frequency Identification

ID	Name	Field	probability Stamp
4711	Manfred	Informatics	0,7
4711	Manfred	Medicine	0,3
1111	Uwe	Math	0,6
1111	Uwe	Sport	0,4

Table 3: Example of tuples in a probabilistic database

The first question is how we will get the probability of each tuple. As [14] describes they can come from e.g. interviews, evaluations, calculations or predictions. An important fact is that a primary key in a probabilistic database cannot longer be unique. Instead the primary key represents exactly one object of an existing world in the database. Therefore at most one tuple of each primary key can be chosen for a possible world. A further condition is that the sum of probabilities of all possible worlds must sum up to 1 [2]. For above example it can be calculated like this:

$$
\left. \begin{array}{l}
P\{\text{Manfred Informatics \& Uwe Math}\} = 0,7*0,6 = 0,42 \\
P\{\text{Manfred Medicine \& Uwe Sport}\} = 0,3*0,4 = 0,12 \\
P\{\text{Manfred Informatics \& Uwe Sport}\} = 0,7*0,4 = 0,28 \\
P\{\text{Manfred Medicine \& Uwe Math}\} = 0,3*0,6 = 0,18
\end{array} \right\} \ 1
$$

These four possibilities are representing all possible worlds for the data in table 3.

4.3 Probability stamp

The column probability stamp (pS) represents the probability that exactly this tuple exists [14]. That means in above example that the probability that a student 4711 with the name Manfred and the field Informatics exists equals 0,6. Through addition of rows it is possible to calculate constrained probabilities [14]. For example P{4711; Manfred} = P{4711; Manfred; Informatics} + P{4711; Manfred; Medicine} = 0,7 + 0,3 = 1. Therefore it is sure that the student 4711 is called Manfred. P{4711; Informatics} = P{4711; Manfred; Informatics} = 0,7 shows that 4711 studies Informatics with a probability of 0,7.

So it is possible through addition of probability values of tuples with same attribute(s) to calculate the possibility of their existence [14].

4.4 Uncertainty of existence

When all possibilities of tuples with the same key sum up to 1 it is sure that this entity exists. In which occurrence is not relevant at this point. But what if the probability values do not sum up to 1? Then it cannot be assumed that this entity exists at all [14]. Table 4 shows this possibility.

ID	Name	Field	pS
4711	Manfred	Informatics	0,3
4711	Uwe	Medicine	0,4

Table 4: Tuple with uncertainty of existence

P{4711} = P{4711; Manfred; Informatics} + P{4711; Uwe; Medicine} = 0,3 + 0,4 = 0,7
Now it is not sure what 4711 studies whether if he even exists! With a probability of 0,3 he
does not exist. There are several reasons a case like this can happen. Maybe this student does
not study anymore or the addition of the tuple was false and this student never existed [14].

4.5 Integrity conditions

Probabilistic databases have to meet different conditions than deterministic databases.
Integrity conditions are divided into intrarelational (valid for a single relation) and referential
(valid for all relations) conditions [14].

Intrarelational integrity conditions

- Each relation has at most one pS-attribute. If there is no pS-attribute it is equal
  to pS = 1 for all tuples
- $pS \in [0,1]$ a value of 0 denotes the non-existence of this tuple, therefore it is
  not stored in the database
- The sum of all pS-values of an object of the real world is not allowed to be
  greater than 1. If the values sum up to 1 the existence of this object is sure.
- No attribute value is allowed to be *NULL* (see 4.6)

Referential integrity conditions

- The sum of pS-values of a foreign-key is not allowed to be greater than the
  sum of pS-values in the referenced table regarding the same primary key.

Let table 5 be the foreign key for the column *field* of table 4. Then it is not allowed that a
student exists studying Informatics with a probability of 0,3 but the probability that
Informatics generally exists is smaller than 0,3. Because the existence of the student
implicates the existence of the field Informatics. Therefore the pS-value of Informatics in
table 5 must be at least 0,3 [14].

Field	City	pS
Informatics	Vienna	0,3
Medicine	Salzburg	0,4

Table 5: Referential integrity

4.6 NULL values

NULL values are very special in informatics. In relational databases they have the meaning of "I don't know" or "doesn't matter" [14]. In principle they stand for an uncertainty. NULL values in probabilistic databases have a similar meaning but in probabilistic databases, as described so far, there is another and more precisely way to handle uncertainties. It's easy to recognize that for data like displayed in table 6 it is not possible to use the concepts mentioned in 4.3.

ID	Name	Field	Year of birth	pS
4711	Manfred	Informatics	1975	0,2
4711	Uwe	Informatics	NULL	0,5
4711	NULL	NULL	1985	0,3

Table 6: Null values in probabilistic databases

If we now want to know the probability that 4711's name is John (P{4711; John}) the only thing we know is that with a probability of 0,2 4711's name is Manfred and with 0,5 Uwe. Therefore with a probability of 0,7 4711's name is not John. Due to the NULL value in row 3 we cannot exclude the possibility that 4711's name is John. So we can only define that the probability must be between 0 and 0,3. That means that P{4711; John} = [0; 0,3]. For example P{4711; Uwe} is then defined with an interval of [0,5; 0,8]. Other predicates:

- P{4711; Informatics} = [0,7; 1]
- P{4711; Name = Informatics; Field = Hugo} = [0; 0,3]
- P{4711; born 500 BC} = [0; 0,5]

In summary it can be said that if NULL values are used in probabilistic databases, the pS-values define upper and lower bounds for the probability [14].

4.7 Conditioning probabilistic data

One essential operation for conditioning probabilistic databases is to remove possible worlds which do not satisfy a given condition [6]. We imagine data read using OCR[6] software where not always every read character can be identified correctly. Therefore different possible worlds will be generated. Table 7 shows a possible example.

---

[6] Online Character Recognition

SSN	Name	pS
1	John	0,2
7	John	0,8
4	Bill	0,3
7	Bill	0,7

Table 7: Example of probabilistic data read using OCR

Here it is easily to see that this data represents four possible worlds:

1. P{1 John & 4 Bill} = 0,2 * 0,3 = 0,06
2. P{7 John & 4 Bill} = 0,8 * 0,3 = 0,24
3. P{1 John & 7 Bill} = 0,2 * 0,7 = 0,14
4. P{7 John & 7 Bill} = 0,8 * 0,7 = 0,56

} 1

As we know social security numbers are generally unique therefore we can add a functional dependency SSN→Name. Asserting this condition results in removing world number 4 of our list. Furthermore as it can be imagined we have to renormalize the possibilities that we can again sum up the possibilities of each world to 1. To do this we have only to divide each remaining world's probability by 0,06 + 0,24 + 0,14 = 0,44 [6].

This shows that conditioning can be reached through adding functional dependency to the database. A problem [6] describes is that conditioning and confidence computing are NP-hard[7] problems.

4.8 Practical scenarios

A solution for a probabilistic database is called MystiQ and can be downloaded at mystiq.cs.washington.edu. There you find also all information about it. As described in this chapter these databases could be used for data integration from different sources or for RFID data management. Unfortunately there are no real examples where such databases are in use. An assumed reason is that the task of getting a probability value for each tuple of a database can take a lot of time. Therefore users have to decide if this effort is worth it. Furthermore probabilisitc databases seem to be still in research due to the fact that most papers were published in the years 2000 till today.

5 Conclusion

In this paper three different applications which are using probabilistic algorithms were presented. In all shown comparisons between them and deterministic variants the former performed better. It must be said that this is not the case under all conditions. Probabilistic algorithms are not the solution for all problems, but it was shown that it is possible to reach

---

[7] nondeterministic polynomial-time hard

better performance with them, mainly in the domains of large scaling networks, whenever decisions have to be done without having complete information and where overall conditions of a system are changing at runtime e.g. the topology of a network.

It came out that the probabilistic influence is differently used at each application. LPBCAST uses the probabilistic factor to calculate the lower bound that a node will receive a disseminated message. This can be controlled by adjusting the value of fanout. At AG the decision of nodes if a gossip request is accepted and whether or not cached gossiping is used is controlled by probability. Furthermore AG uses probability to decide if gossiping is done with a distant node or with a locally node. At probabilistic routing PRoPHET uses probability to calculate if another node is suitable to transfer a message to the target node. Epidemic routing itself is as mentioned not a real probabilistic routing protocol, in spite of this fact there is also a probabilistic factor because a node receives a message only probably. Entirely different behave probabilistic databases. There probability is used to rank queries and build possible worlds. Differently than probabilistic routing or broadcasting the probability values are not calculated but have to be evaluated through interviews, predictions or otherwise. This evaluation of probabilities is a hard task.

Also for probabilistic routing and broadcasting initial probability values have to be set, but due to the fact that they change during runtime they are not as essential as they are for probabilistic databases. For routing and broadcasting protocols the parameter values are more important than the initial probabilistic values because they are used to control them. Therefore different applications use the probabilistic factor in a different way for reaching their goals.

Bibliography

[1] R. Chandra, V. Ramasubramanian, and K. Birman. *Anonymous gossip: Improving multicast reliability in mobile adhoc networks*. In Proc. 21st International Conference on Distributed Computing Systems (ICDCS), 2001.

[2] N. Dalvi, D.Suciu, *Management of Probabilistic Data Foundations and Challenges*, Proceedings of the twenty-sixth ACM SIGMOD-SIGACT-SIGART symposium on Principles of database systems, p.1-12, June 11-13, 2007, Beijing, China

[3] Th. Eugster, R.Guerraoui, S.B. Handurukande, P.Kouznetsov, A.-M. Kermarrec, *Lightweight Probabilistic Broadcast*, ACM Transactions on Computer Systems, Vol. 21, No. 4, November 2003, Pages 341–374.

[4] Johnson, D.B., Maltz, D.A.: *Dynamic source routing in ad hoc wireless networks*. In Imielinski, Korth, eds.: Mobile Computing. Volume 353. Kluwer Academic Publishers (1996) 153–181

[5] Khambatti, M., Ryu, K., Dasgupta, P., *Push-Pull Gossiping for Information Sharing in Peer-to-Peer Communities*, In Int'l Conf. on Parallel and Distributed Processing Techniques and Applications (PDPTA), (Las Vegas, NV, 2003)

[6] C. Koch, D. Olteanu, *Conditioning Probabilistic Databases*, In Proc. VLDB, 2008.

[7] A. Lindgren, A. Doria, O. Schelen, *Probabilistic Routing in Intermittently Connected Networks*, SAPIR 2004, LNCS 3126, pp. 239–254, 2004, Springer Verlag, Berlin Heidelberg 2004

[8] D.Maier; *Gossiping*, Diplomarbeit, 2003/2004 ETH Zürich

[9] Josyula R. Rao, *Reasoning about Probabilistic Algorithms*, Proceedings of the ninth annual ACM symposium on Principles of distributed computing, p.247-264, August 22-24, 1990, Quebec City, Quebec, Canada

[10] Christopher Re, Dan Suciu, *Management of Data with Uncertainities*, CIKM'07, November 6–8, 2007, Lisboa, Portugal.

[11] E.M.Royer and C.E.Perkins, *Multicast Operation of the Ad-hoc On-Demand Distance Vector Routing Protocol*, In Mobile Computing and Networking, 1999

[12] A.S.Tanenbaum, M.Van Steen, *Distributed Systems*, Second Edition, Page 171, Pearson Education, New Jersey, 2007

[13] A. Vahdat, D. Becker, *Epidemic Routing for Partially-Connected Ad Hoc Networks*, Duke Tech Report CS-2000-06, 2000

[14] Maarten van Hoek, *Probabilistische Datenbanken*, Seminar Intelligente Datenbanken, 2005

List of Figures

List of Tables

List of Abbreviations

AG   Anonymous Gossiping

ER   Epidemic Routing

LPBCAST   Lightweight Probabilistic Broadcast

MRT   Multicast Routing Table

pS   Probability stamp

RT   Route Table